it's kind of FUN TO DO THE IMPOSSIBLE

-Walt Disney

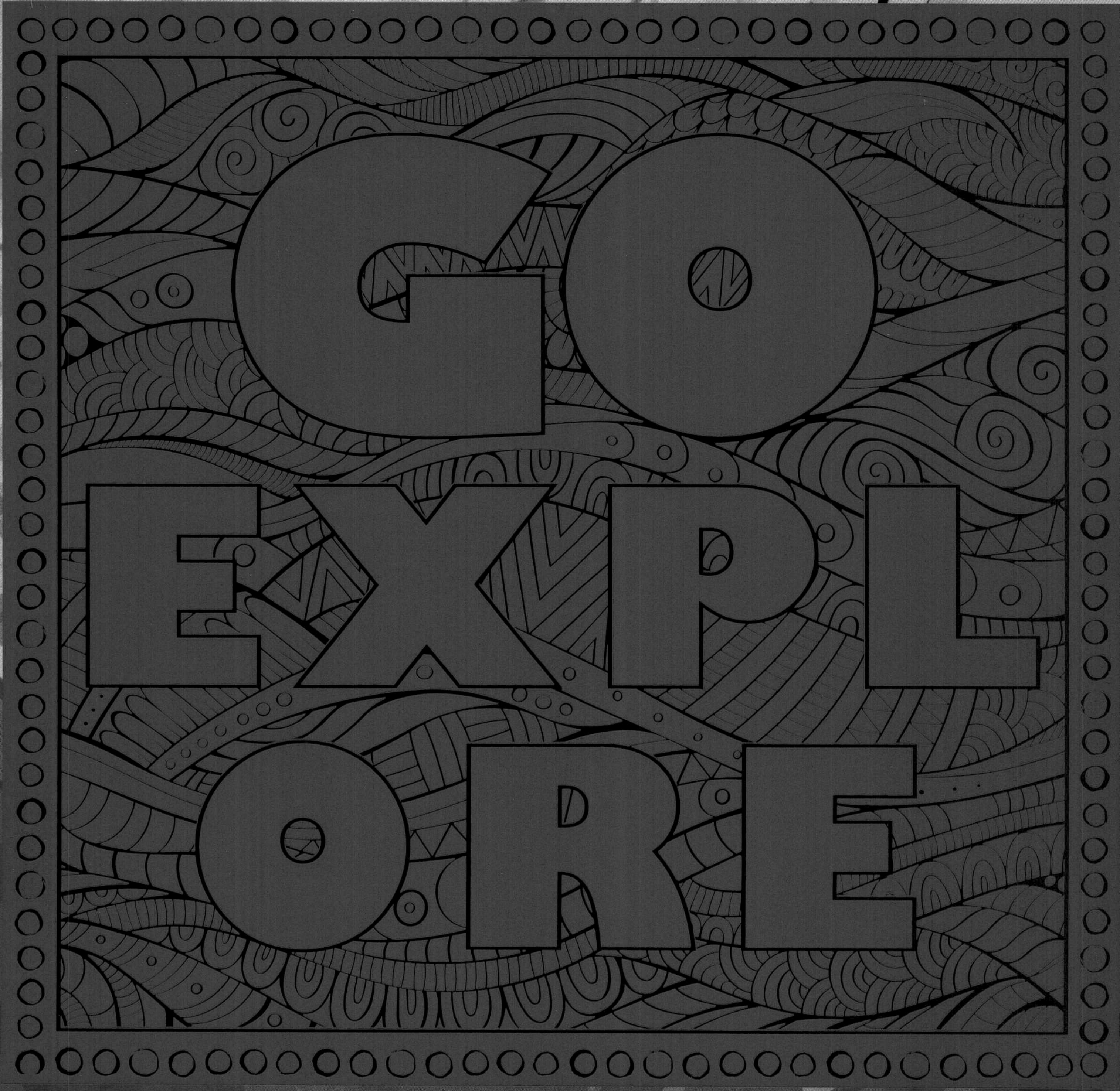
GO
EXPLORE

you are
ENTIRELY
UP TO
YOU

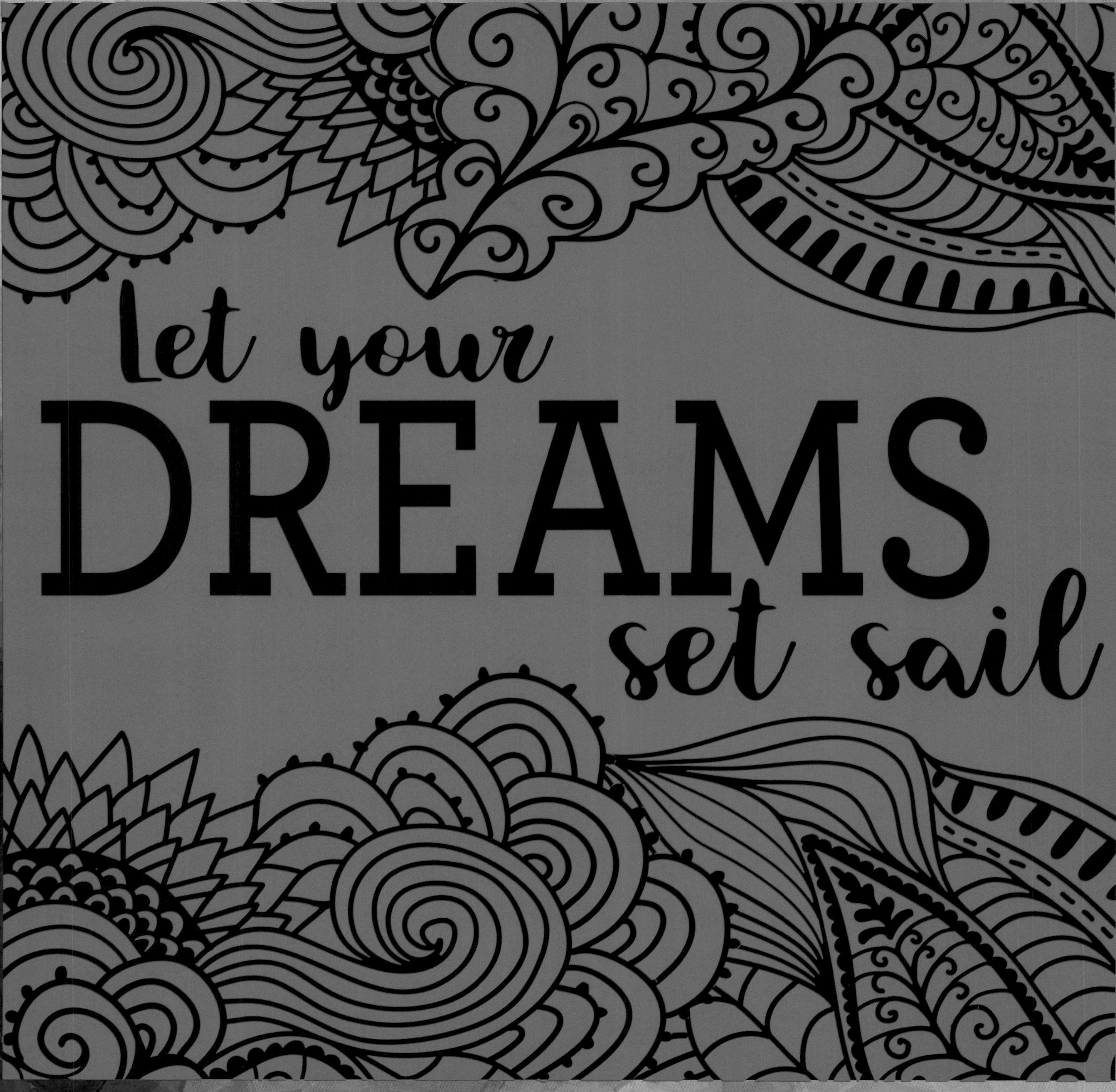
Let your
DREAMS
set sail